Silence in the Storm

AF624563

Jacqueline Gonzalez

BookLeaf Publishing

Silence in the Storm © 2023 Jacqueline Gonzalez

All rights reserved.

No part of this publication may be reproduced, stored in a retrieval system, or transmitted, in any form or by any means, electronic, mechanical, photocopying, recording or otherwise, without the prior written permission of the presenters.

Jacqueline Gonzalez asserts the moral right to be identified as author of this work.

Presentation by *BookLeaf Publishing*

Web: www.bookleafpub.com

E-mail: info@bookleafpub.com

ISBN: 9789357212328

First edition 2023

DEDICATION

To Marco, Josef, and Isabella

ACKNOWLEDGEMENT

Thank you to my husband, Marco, and my children, Josef and Isabella, for having faith in me and always encouraging me to write. In addition, a huge thanks to the entire faculty at Southern New Hampshire's Graduate English department for helping me develop my creative writing skills, and of course, to BookLeaf Publishing for this amazing opportunity.

The Wilted Rose

Have you heard about the wilted rose,
That stands still every day?
The wind from the storm growls with all its
might,
But still it doesn't blow away.

It continues to lose its vibrant color,
As its petals turn a dark shade of brown.
But no matter how hard the rain falls,
It still won’t tumble down.

The burst of petals once stood tall,
Each one colored a bright blood red.
If anyone touched the stem protected by thorns,
Surely they stood there and bled.

As time passed, the rose lost its beauty,
And each thorn was picked away.
There was nothing left to protect it,
And it began to wither more and more each day.

Those who remember the vibrance of the rose,
Try to revive it every possible way.
But until the right remedy comes along,
It will continue to fade away.

Precious Misery

They say misery loves company,
But you're all the way over there.
You've done nothing but make me miserable,
But of course, you simply don't care.

You made it seem like there were sparks,
And that we were meant to be.
But I guess it was only fun and games,
And now all that's left is me.

Lucky for you I'm used to being alone,
So please be on your way.
Because now I've completely erased you,
And there's nothing more to say.

What Good is a Smile?

What good is a smile,
When it comes from a stranger?
Soon, they'll be gone in a while,
And I'll be back to my anger.

What good is a smile,
When it comes from a relative?
If their efforts are forced,
And everything they say and do is negative.

What good is a smile,
When it comes from a friend?
If they promised to be there,
But are always gone in the end?

And what good is a smile,
When it comes from your own reflection?
If its only a show for the world,
And nothing but false projection.

If Tonight is My Last...

If tonight is my last on earth.
I know I did all I could do.
To show you how deep my love runs,
But the rest is up to you.

I should've trusted my instincts,
And run like hell that day.
But instead I stuck around,
And allowed myself to be your prey.

The strength of your lies,
Was no match for the strength of my pride.
But somehow, the warmth of your smile,
Was the reason a part inside of me died.

But if an angel came down on my last day,
And the sky threatened to crash down on me.
I would change nothing at all,
Since losing you finally set me free.

Liquid Remedy

Whiskey burns, and tequila stings.
But nothing else compares,
To the cold heartache that you bring.

Vodka is spicy, and wine is dry.
I should have known by your demeanor,
That every word you spewed was just a lie.

Beer is tart and rum is sweet.
Doesn't matter what you did to me,
In no time I'll be back on my feet.

So, as I sit here, a margarita I shall pour.
As I toast to your absence,
While breathing happily over the newly closed
door.

Beautiful Rising

Keep your chin up, princess,
The world is yours for the taking.
The skies turn a beautiful bright blue,
In anticipation for your awakening.

The sun shines brightly,
As the moon goes to sleep.
So now it's your chance,
To let go of all fear and take that major leap.

Don't let past mistakes
Be your misdirection.
So, stand up tall,
And forget all your imperfections.

The goals laid out before you,
Aren't anything you can't achieve.
Close your ears to the haters,
In yourself you must believe.

Now it's time to stand up tall,
And adjust your pretty crown.
Because the world is ready for you,
So don't let it or yourself down.

Phantom Silhouette

The one that used to comfort me when I felt all alone,
Is now a ghost that has found its way into another home.
The way it used to haunt my dreams, it often brought me comfort.
But now that it's gone, I have no reason to make any further effort.

Now, the eerie sound in this wide and empty space,
Channels every echo like a cold embrace.
And the apparition that I pretend to see,
Is simply my vanishing reflection staring back at me.

Is this what crazy feels like - am I going downhill?
I thought I had it figured out, but its presence was just a drill.
If it was meant to be, I would not feel this way.
So I must say goodbye to this supernatural force - because I know it'll never stay.

Manic Desire

He saw her walking across the room one day,
Flipping her long brown hair.
And he felt a chill run down his spine,
Knowing that no other woman could compare.

Those bright red lips and big brown eyes,
Made him say and do crazy things.
He wanted nothing more than to be with her,
But he knew the danger that rejection could
bring.

He bit the bullet and made the first move,
But they only became great friends.
He still couldn't shake the feeling that there
might be more-
The possibility of a great love that would never
end.

But he'll never get the chance, you see -
For she belongs to another.
Although he feels his heart's been ripped out,
He'll continue to love her like no other.

Mirror, Mirror on the Wall

Mirror, mirror on the wall,
Who is the greatest one of all?
My dear girl, you it could never be,
Since you are just as clueless and ignorant as he.

You're full on his garbage, and you believe all his deceit.
Even though you know with you he only intends to cheat.
He tells you that you're amazing and only you will do.
Yet, he goes home to the only woman he loves, not to you.

But mirror, mirror on the wall,
Do you think he could eventually love me, after all?
My dear girl, did you not hear a word I said?
For the man you love is too insecure and afraid.

No matter how beautiful, intelligent, and successful you are,
There will always be someone else catching his glimpse from afar.
While you sit here dwelling on what could be,

He’s thinking of a new batch of lies for his next cheating spree.

Mirror, mirror on the wall….
Hush, my dear girl, don’t say anything else, at all-

I'm Fine, Save Me

Today I am sending smiles all around,
Maybe tomorrow I'll have a frown.
I just Figure that if I breath deep enough,
It will remind me that I can be tough.
It's Not as bad as it could be, really,
Even though I struggle, I'll be fine, you'll see.

But Silent storms are rolling in my heart,
And they're developing into a hurricane, tearing me apart.
Violent and thieving of the saner parts of me,
Everything is pointing to me never being set free.
Maybe I'm not as fine as I originally thought,
Especially since this is the toughest battle I've ever fought.

A Woman's Plight

They say you're too fat,
And that you need to lose weight.
But when you do, you're too skinny,
And need to add more food to your plate.

If you wear too much makeup,
Then you're clearly an attention seeking whore.
But if you don't wear any or enough,
Then you're just a basic bitch who's nothing but a bore.

Your wear fake eyelashes and a push-up bra,
So you must be catfishing.
But if you bring up their beards and large trucks,
You're just deflecting and bitching.

Your hair is too long,
And you look a hot mess.
But then they complain it's too short,
And you look like a boy in that dress.

Your body is constantly on display,
For men to gawk and observe.
But rather than appreciate it,
They hurl insults that you don't deserve.

Oh - and don't talk about bodily autonomy,
Because somehow it's their body too.
Women's rights is nothing but a myth,
And your next move will never entirely be up to you.

They don't care about anything you have to say,
Even though you demonstrate nothing but class.
All they expect from you is silent obedience,
Oh, but be sure to wear that short dress that perfectly shows your ass.

The irony of it all is that if you speak up for yourself,
You're a raging bitch that needs to be put in her place.
But if you're silent and obedient -
You'll bore them enough to find someone else to chase.

As we stand tall and proud of who are are, we ask:
What is it that you want from us?
Should we stay quiet and let you assert control,
And just let you do your thing and not make a fuss?

Let's be honest, no matter what we do,

You'll always find something that to you is worth complaining-
Because your idea of what or who a woman should be,
You'll only ever find through instilling fear by being controlling.

But the joke is on you, since we know our worth,
And we refuse to be a female robot or an obedient slave.
So, kindly turn and find the nearest exit; there's nothing here for you,
Because now we stand on our own two feet - strong, self-loving, and brave.

Silent Wishes

The sun is yellow.
The moon is white.
But all I can do is think about you,
Tonight.

The skies are blue.
The clouds are gray.
But all I can do is hope that you're thinking of
me,
Today.

The rain is cold.
The wind blows strong.
But all I can do is wish that you truly loved me,
All along.

The Hostile Escape

The room is cold and eerie,
Her blood is on the table.
She tries to regain her strength,
But she is just not able.

Through tear stained eyes she sees the knife,
And tries to crawl in that direction.
For she has only one goal,
And that's to use it for protection.

Every move she makes is silent,
So she doesn't let him know,
That he hasn't succeeded in killing her,
But her anger is starting to grow.

He's staring out the window,
While sipping on a beer.
Becuase he thinks that he has killed her,
So he doesn't feel her coming near.

She grabs the knife off the floor,
And wipes her blood away.
And feels the force of a thousand angels,
Giving her strength today.

The wincing pain from each stab wound,
For a moment makes her lose control.
But somehow she keeps crawling,
Towards the man who damaged her soul.

She slowly lifts herself off the floor,
And moves herself closer his way.
For he's in the perfect place - the window -
And his murderous game, she's ready to play.

He chugs the rest of his beer and lets out a
menacing laugh,
While reveling in his murderous success.
But he's shocked when he turns around and sees
The woman he thought he killed, who is ready to
make a mess.

Standing still, he glares at her with a smug grin,
Until he sees the blood, oozing from his chest,
grasping it in pain.
He starts to lunge at her, only driving the knife
further.
And now it's her turn to smile - he'll never hurt
her again.

Daddy's Betrayal

A beer bottle breaks,
The little boy cries.
He hears his daddy yelling,
Shortly after, his mommy dies.

The yells and the screams,
Frightened the little boy.
But all he wanted was his mom to wake up,
And take him away from all the noise.

His mommy laid still in a pool of blood,
His daddy standing over her body.
The boy said softly, “mommy wake up,”
But he knew it was too late - she was too bloody.

His daddy dropped to his knees,
And let out a loud cry.
"I didn’t mean to hurt your mommy."
"I didn’t mean for her to die."

"I wanted her to be quiet,
But she wouldn’t stop yelling."
"Now I can’t take anything back,
And it’s all overwhelming."

The damage was done, and there was nothing
more to do.
"Please forgive me, boy," his daddy said,
But the little boy would never forget -
That because of his daddy, his mommy was
dead.

A Young Woman Left for Dead

Eyes lined with purple and black,
Her lips a striking blood red.
A tear stained face and a broken heart,
A young woman left for dead.

She lay still on the floor,
As the color drained from her face.
He tried to hold her close,
But he was met with a cold embrace.

Her eyes wouldn't open,
No movement in her body.
He tried holding her hand,
And received cold stares from everybody.

He didn't mean to swing so hard,
But he couldn't take it back.
He stared at her lifeless body,
As his entire existence faded to black.

I'm a Loaded Gun

If you choose to pull my trigger,
Just know that I'm a loaded gun.
So please tread carefully, or you'll discover,
that my wrath has only just begun.

I walk with a calm demeanor,
And fool people with every smile.
Since I'm really just a ticking time bomb,
And when pushed, I turn extremely vile.

Abuse is just a word to you,
But to me it's been my whole life.
So if you choose to try to hurt me,
Be careful, because my words cut like a knife.

The thought of losing you in my life,
On me has no effect.
Because I'm used to people leaving,
And treating me with neglect.

But I guess there's still some good in me,
Since I'm issuing this warning.
So don't say you didn't know what to expect,
Because you knew exactly what was coming.

My bullets may in the form of harsh words,
But I'll wound you with each one.
So like I said before, if you choose to pull my trigger,
Just know that I'm a loaded gun.

Bittersweet Eclipse

She gave him love as though her last day was
tomorrow,
But he didn't care for her efforts, and left her to
drown in sorrow.

Their relationship had definitely seen better
days,
But all he cared about was indulging in his
philandering ways.

She thought her allure had vanished, and if she
changed he might return,
But that would never happen, because that
bridge, he decided to burn.

She moved on and used her strength to hold her
still.
But no matter how hard she tried, her heart
wasn't ready to climb up that hill.

She yearned for his return and waited for a visit,
a call, or a text.
But when he refused to make contact with her,
she was shocked at what she'd be doing next.

She found him with a younger woman, who
wasn't worth the trouble or the pain.
But then again, his entire life was in shambles,
and falling down the drain.

She fought like hell to make him come home,
which only kept him away longer,
And now she's done fighting for him, and as
time goes on she's getting stronger.

How did she give up so easily, you might ask,
But trust me, for her, letting go was no simple
task.

She looked around at everything she would gain,
If she said goodbye and never saw him again.

She saw the stars align and life finally made
sense,
And she no longer had to suffer at her own
expense.

You'll Never Be Enough

Lips too red.
Eyelashes too long.
It's tough to be a woman in a man's world;
Everything you do is wrong.

Looking for your place in the world,
Means standing small next to a group of men.
But be careful not to complain too much,
It's an argument you'll never win.

They view women like a sampler platter,
At their favorite restaurant's buffet.
And when the first plate is gone,
They're ready for another helping of feminine
array.

If you withhold sex from them,
They call you a tease.
But if you willingly give yourself,
Then they think being with you is a breeze.

Don't think they'll be faithful, though,
Just because you were willing.
There will always be another woman,

Because whatever the men want, they are fulfilling.

Her Hot Pink Journal

She flips through the blank pages,
Of her new hot pink journal.
Digging for the right words,
To describe a love eternal.

She looked for inspiration,
In all the wrong places
Because the one she fell for,
Fooled her with his many faces.

The lies that she fell for,
Are now her driving force.
They should have broken her heart,
But now it's all just run its course.

The sweet words that she looked for,
Were replaced with bold faced lies.
But in hindsight it was a blessing,
Before she fell for his disguise.

She's doing a lot better now,
And brave and tall she'll stand.
For the love eternal she thought she found,
Was nothing like she'd planned.

Now she's finally found the perfect spot,
And she's ready to write about it all.
On the blank pages she was flipping through,
Of her new hot pink journal.

The 7 Deadly Men

Lust sees a beautiful flower that belongs to someone else,
And is instantly filled with desires to keep it for himself.
While the many flowers building up in Greed's flower bed,
are never enough to keep him happy and ahead.
Gluttony is starving for every new flower and its seeds,
Which makes him no better than that selfish monster, Greed.
Sloth has a flower in his room, but he's too lazy to care,
So the flower shrivels up and dies, leaving him in despair.
Envy becomes angry with everyone who gets a new flower,
And feels that no one but he should add more to their power.
The rage that fills Wrath guarantees that havoc he'll wreak,
Leaving any flower that crosses his path, wilted and weak.
But pride is the biggest demon of all,

Because he loves the flower, but in love, he won't allow himself to fall.

If My Eyes Could Take Pictures...

If my eyes could take pictures,
Oh, the things that you would see.
Because I'm so very observant,
And you'd see the world through me.

You would notice the beauty of the ocean,
And its refreshing shade of blue.
You'd also see the tall green trees,
And wonder what without them you would do.

The picture of love that my photos would capture,
To you would be an anomaly.
But if you'd just focus, you'd see how beautiful,
My version of love could truly be.

You'd see my children smiling,
About the most trivial things.
But you'd also see their humility,
And how they treasure all that life brings.

You'd look at pictures of the night sky above,
And maybe wish upon a star.
You'll value your life differently,

And realize you're perfect just the way you are.

So now that you have seen life through my eyes,
Maybe you'll have a different view.
And if you're ever having a bad day,
Just think of all the beauty surrounding you.

www.ingramcontent.com/pod-product-compliance
Lightning Source LLC
Chambersburg PA
CBHW051749130826
49812CB00033B/1061
* 9 7 8 9 3 5 7 2 1 2 3 2 8 *